FRONTISPIECE: Medallion portrait of Captain James Cook by Josiah Wedgwood, from a design by John Flaxman, 1784

Captain James Cook—
after two hundred years

A commemorative address
delivered before the Hakluyt Society
by R. A. SKELTON

Published by the Trustees of the British Museum

LONDON 1969

PRINTED IN GREAT BRITAIN
AT THE UNIVERSITY PRESS, OXFORD
BY VIVIAN RIDLER
PRINTER TO THE UNIVERSITY

This address was delivered before the Hakluyt Society in the Beveridge Hall, University of London, on 18 July 1968, with the President of the Society, Sir Gilbert Laithwaite, in the chair. It formed part of the bicentenary exercises commemorating the beginning of Captain James Cook's first voyage round the world, 1768–71.

Quotations from Cook's journals in the text are made, without reference in the notes, from Dr. J. C. Beaglehole's edition, *The Journals of Captain James Cook on his Voyages of Discovery*, Vols. I–III (Hakluyt Society, 1955–67). To this landmark in historical scholarship the author, in common with all students of Cook, owes an immeasurable debt.

Illustrations

6

The design on the cover shows the decoration of Maori canoe paddles, in a wash and water-colour drawing, perhaps by J. F. Miller (B.M., Add. MS. 23920.71a).

Acknowledgements

Reproductions of subjects not in the British Museum are made by courtesy of the Trustees of the National Maritime Museum (I, X, XIV, XVI), the Trustees of the British Museum (Natural History) (XXIII, XXIV), the Controller of H.M. Stationery Office (XII, XIX), the Hydrographer of the Navy (II, XV), and the Librarian, National Library of Australia (IV). Blocks for pl. IV, VI–VIII, X, XI, XIII, XIV, XVI, and XXIII were kindly lent by the President and Council of the Hakluyt Society.

Captain James Cook—after two hundred years

IN THE TITLE of my lecture there is one unnecessary word. Cook, like Johnson, is one of the commonest of English surnames; yet for two hundred years the world has talked of Dr. Johnson and of Captain Cook without feeling the need for specific identification by Christian name. The testimony of contemporaries and of his earliest biographers shows that the eighteenth century was as convinced of Cook's greatness as we are in the twentieth; they searched for superlatives. In his own lifetime it was said that he 'will go down to posterity as one of our principal discoverers'.[1] After his death, men of some sophistication who had sailed with him acknowledged 'his powerful and comprehensive genius'[2] and perceived him 'to have been one of the greatest men of his age'.[3] The legend chosen by Admiral Palliser for the first memorial to Cook (still standing at Vache Park) commemorated 'this great Master of his profession, whose skill and labours have enlarged natural philosophy [and] extended nautical Science'.[4] David Samwell, one of Cook's surgeons, wrote in 1786: 'England has been unanimous in her tribute of applause to his virtues, and all Europe has borne testimony to his merit.'[5]

With these tributes, confirmed by a large and still growing literature, we may compare a twentieth-century historian's assessment of Cook as 'the greatest explorer of his age, the greatest maritime explorer of his country in any age'.[6]

It is not uncommon to find that, the more we learn about a Hero, the less we know about the Man. 'Others abide our question, thou art free', as a slogan, does not help us far towards understanding what made a man tick. Andrew Kippis, Cook's first biographer, produced a useful (if rather pompous) book, but he started on the wrong foot. 'A narrative of the Life and Actions of Captain Cook', he wrote, 'must

9

principally consist of the voyages and discoveries he made, and the difficulties and dangers to which he was exposed. . . . His public transactions are the things that mark the man, that display his mind and character . . .' Kippis here shows a healthy awareness that the work is a function of personality; it is a pity that he was blind to the light that knowledge of personality, in its more intimate manifestations, can throw on the work. How much we must regret that he did not use his opportunities to uncover more of what he calls 'the private incidents concerning [Cook]', about the personal relationships and the ordinary qualities, developed to a high degree, that went to make up an extraordinary man! Why did he not extract more from Mrs. Cook ('the Captain's amiable and worthy Widow', as he terms her), who gave him 'an account of several domestic circumstances'? We discover from Kippis a good deal about what Cook did, very little about what he was. In Dr. Beaglehole's words, 'everybody knows Cook's name; yet . . . extraordinarily little is known about him. He is an exceptionally difficult man to get inside.'[7]

Some legitimate questions may be asked about the *personalia* of famous men. 'And did you once see Shelley plain? . . . What porridge ate John Keats?' They are questions which may and should be asked, not only about a creative artist, but (no less) about a man of action whose work has made significant contributions to natural and physical science.

A great man is not a mere hiccup in history. He is, like Cook, a child of his time—but one who, through mastery of its techniques of thought and action won by force of intellect and character, significantly diverts or retards or accelerates the historical process. Cook as a man, and as a man of the eighteenth century, is a proper subject for study.

These rather sententious observations will, as we survey Cook's career, suggest some troublesome questions. They may add a few details to the ground-plan for a revaluation of the man and his achievement. The architect of the building must surely be the scholar who has laid its foundations by enabling us to read (so far as the limitations of print allow) exactly what Cook wrote about his three Pacific voyages, and to glimpse the processes of thought which went into the writing.

Two hundred years ago today, the pilot came on board H.M. Bark *Endeavour*, commanded by Lieutenant James Cook, then lying in the basin of Deptford Dockyard. On 27 May Cook had 'hoisted the Pendant and took charge of the Ship agreable to my Commission of the 25th Instant'. The first entry of his holograph Journal continues: 'From this day to the 21st of July we were constantly occupied in fitting the Ship takeing on board stores and Provisions &c^{a}.' On 21 July the pilot took the ship down Thames to Galleons Reach, and thence by stages to the Downs. Here he was sent ashore on 7 August and Cook took charge of her, to sail for Plymouth next day.

The pedestrian record of routine preparation of a ship for sea, in the commander's journal and the *Endeavour*'s log, is the prelude to the career in geographical discovery, lasting ten years, by which Cook printed his name on the pages of history. At this turning-point in his life, which we commemorate today, we need to look back as well as forward, always remembering that Cook himself seldom indulged in retrospection except for severely practical purposes.

Early in April 1768 (the exact date is uncertain), James Cook had been selected by the Admiralty to command the ship which was to take the Royal Society's observers, one of whom was Cook himself, to Tahiti for astronomical observations. She was to carry other scientific passengers, but Cook's secret instructions had political and economic overtones. The Admiralty had 'reason to imagine that a Continent or Land of great extent, may be found' in the South Pacific Ocean;[8] and no government could be indifferent (in Alexander

Dalrymple's words) to 'such an accession of commerce and power as the discovery of a New World would afford'.[9] The *Endeavour*'s expedition was an act of national policy. Her commander (to quote J. A. Williamson's romantic phrase) bore 'in his capable hands not only the interests of science but the fortunes of his country'.[10]

What kind of man did the Admiralty look for, and get, for this important service? Expeditions sent out with similar instructions during the previous five years had been commanded by a commodore and by two captains respectively. The appointment to the *Endeavour* was not even filled from the list of commissioned officers; it went to a warrant officer of eleven years' seniority in his rating as Master. Their Lordships must have seen uncommon qualities in him. What do we know of Cook in 1768?

At this point we must be struck by a certain lack of balance in the published literature on Cook. This impression may be partly subjective; I confess an immoderate admiration for the Surveyor of Newfoundland. But there are perhaps more solid grounds. To begin with, quantitatively. When Cook was commissioned to *Endeavour*, he was $39\frac{1}{2}$ years old, with $21\frac{1}{2}$ years of service at sea behind him, and only $10\frac{1}{2}$ years of life remaining. In Kippis's biography, only eleven pages in about 530 are given to the first three-quarters of Cook's life; in Kitson's, eighty out of 500 pages; in Carrington's, forty out of 300.[11] The interest in Cook's early life, though still unimpressive, has increased as the sources for it recede in time. Then, qualitatively. In a man's fortieth year, it is generally possible to estimate, from his performance, his immediate capacity and (beyond this) his power of growth—or, as we might say today, to determine his potential ceiling. That is, if we are judging him on ability alone. With the advantage of hindsight, we can without difficulty concede the inspired rightness of the Admiralty's choice, though they may well have been startled by the powers of development that Cook showed during the Pacific voyages, and especially on the first. Let us admit that it calls for an effort of imagination to recognize the surveyor of Newfoundland in the commander who in July 1771 returned from the Pacific with (in Dr. Beaglehole's words) 'a greatly heightened sense of the scope of human thought'.[12] It is very much easier to see the commander of the *Endeavour* in the man who took the *Resolution*, in 1773–4, three times across the South Pacific Ocean and twice over the Antarctic Circle and, in 1778, through Bering Strait and into the Arctic Sea.

It is evident, I think, that the Lords of the Admiralty knew Cook in 1768 a good deal better than we now do. It is not so certain that the documentation available for Cook's early life, up to 1768, has been fully exploited. We may hope that Dr. Beaglehole's projected biography will throw light into its darker corners and portray in sharper definition the man before he became a hero.

It is of course true that, in eighteenth-century England, merit alone did not necessarily bring advancement. The Royal Navy was one of the more democratic British institutions in this respect, particularly perhaps after Lord Anson's tenure of the office of First Lord (1751–61). Still, it has been said— 'not altogether untruthfully', in Professor Michael Lewis's view[13]—that, to reach the top of his profession, an eighteenth-century naval officer needed three qualifications: influence with the right people, ability, and regular employment in a time of warfare. In the last two of these conditions, Cook was well endowed, and by 1768 they had brought him a measure of interest in the corridors of power—far greater, it is clear, than that of many contemporaries with superior advantages of birth, education, or family connection.

Explicit testimony to the growing regard in which James Cook was held by authority crops up intermittently, but regularly and effectively, in the course of his early career at sea. In 1755, just before enlisting in the Navy, he was offered command of a Whitby merchant ship by Captain John Walker, the Quaker ship-owner in whose service he had been since his nineteenth year. Captain Hugh Palliser, under whose command Cook served in the English Channel in 1755–7, was to become Governor of Newfoundland (in 1763), Comptroller of the Navy, and a Lord of the Admiralty. Captain John Simcoe commanded H.M.S. *Pembroke*, a ship-of-the-line, in the Gulf of St. Lawrence in 1757–9, when Cook was her master, and made a contribution to his professional career which is not less significant for being almost unnoticed. He encouraged Cook's study of mathematics and astronomy and his early exercises in hydrographic survey; we are also told that he 'mentioned to several of his friends in power, the necessity of having surveys of these parts and astronomical observations made as soon as peace was restored'. The recorder of this episode, the military engineer Samuel Holland, adds that Cook, when they met in London in 1776, 'candidly confessed that the several improvements and instructions he had received on board the *Pembroke* had been the sole foundation of the services he had been enabled to perform'.[14]

Here we are led on to the Newfoundland survey. After three years' service as master of H.M.S. *Northumberland*, under Commodore Lord Colville, Cook was paid off in September 1762. Two months later, Colville wrote to the Admiralty recommending Cook's charts and sailing directions and informing 'their lordships, that from my experience of Mr Cook's genius and capacity, I think him well fitted for the work he has undertaken, and for greater undertakings of the same kind'. This letter was perhaps prompted by Commodore Thomas Graves, the newly appointed naval Governor of Newfoundland. In March 1763 Graves, having doubtless prepared the ground, simultaneously moved the Board of Trade to approve the appointment of a hydrographic surveyor, and the Board of Admiralty to nominate Cook to the post. During the five years of the Newfoundland survey, the correspondence repeatedly illustrates the confidence of the Governor—first Graves, then Palliser—in his surveyor, and also Cook's self-possession in his dealings with men in high position. He is the Governor's emissary in delivering his charts to the Admiralty; he reports in person to the Chancellor of the Exchequer and the First Lord of the Admiralty; he searches the London map-shops, on Palliser's behalf, for evidence on French fishing rights; the Governor persuades the Admiralty to authorize the printing of Cook's charts. In 1766 the astronomer John Bevis communicates Cook's observations of a solar eclipse to the Royal Society and describes him as 'a good mathematician, and very expert in his business' (of hydrographic surveying). So Cook was becoming known to admirals, politicians, and scientists.

This crescendo of commendation makes the commissioning of Cook to the *Endeavour* seem almost a foregone conclusion. To a large extent it explains why the Admiralty thought him competent to execute their plan for the voyage. It does not tell us fully or precisely what was Cook's intellectual and moral equipment for his new task of geographical exploration, nor how much his previous experience moulded his performance in this task, nor how he was able to execute his instructions with a thoroughness and generosity which went far beyond the results of previous voyages and (surely) the expectations of the Admiralty.

We shall do well to remember that it was one and the same man who, as a merchant seaman, was employed for nine years in the North Sea and Scandinavian trades; who served, for another seven and a half years, as mate and master in ships-of-the-line engaged in naval operations, mainly in North America; who spent five years on a systematic marine survey of the coasts of Newfoundland—and who was to uncover the geography of the Pacific Ocean. Each of the earlier phases of his life must have been formative. To the Pacific and to the Polar Regions Cook brought with him traits of character, professional habits, and mental images formed between his nineteenth and his fortieth year, that is before 1768.

When we look for specific evidence of this, Cook himself does not help us much. His Pacific journals yield very few clear reflections of his sea-going experience in the waters of northern Europe and of north-eastern North America. For the expeditions to the Pacific he requisitioned the same instruments with which the Newfoundland survey had been made. He also took some of the same men. Most of the *Grenville*'s small crew were mustered in the *Endeavour*. On the Newfoundland survey, too, the *Grenville* carried local fishermen temporarily on her strength 'to point out hidden dangers'; [15] here was a precedent for the three Tahitians who appear in the *Endeavour*'s muster-books in the summer of 1769, as supernumeraries, to act as 'Guides for the interior Parts of the Island & Pilots for the Coast'.

Local informants also supplied indigenous place names. On one of his manuscript charts of the north coast of Newfoundland, Cook wrote down 'A Table of the names of the places . . . as they are known to the English and French' fishermen. In Tonga, in 1777, William Anderson, surgeon of the *Resolution*, 'procur'd names of above a hundred and twenty islands'. Between Cook's practice in bestowing new place names in Newfoundland and in the Pacific there are repeated parallels and echoes. The descriptive toponymy most clearly betrays what was in his mind's eye. For instance,

the names 'Bay of Islands' and 'River Thames', both bestowed by Cook in Newfoundland, were also applied by him
to features in New Zealand—with a reminiscence of the flood-
tide below London Bridge and of the marshy lower reaches
of the English Thames. Thrum Cap (meaning a bonnet of
tow looking like a mop) is the name of a low wooded island
at the mouth of Halifax Harbour (Nova Scotia), which Cook
had charted in 1762. It was, I suppose, the aspect of this
island which came back to his memory in April 1769, when
he sighted an atoll in the Tuamotu Archipelago which
'prov'd to be a low woody Island of a circular form'.

His second and third voyages took Cook into high latitudes
where he could draw on observations of ice conditions and
of sub-Arctic fauna and flora from his experience before 1768.
In the discussion of Antarctic sea-ice, in his journal for 1775,
we find allusions to the winter freezing of the sea in the Baltic,
Gulf of St. Lawrence, and Belle Isle Strait; and on the north-
west coast of North America, in 1778, recollections of the
walruses or 'sea-cows' in the St. Lawrence and of Newfoundland plants which he noticed in the Aleutians. The making
of spruce beer and its virtues as an antiscorbutic (unknown
in England before the American Revolutionary War) were
almost certainly learnt by Cook in Nova Scotia or Newfoundland.[16]

These straws of Cook's own testimony, however you twist
them, do not make a very strong cord of continuity. It can
be reinforced by reasonable inference from unmistakable,
though less explicit, parallels in the record.

Dr. Johnson, in a facetious conversation with Boswell in 1772,
explained why he 'laid aside' his temptation to sail with Cook
in the *Resolution*. To begin with, he was too shortsighted; and
then, as he averred, 'there is very little of intellectual, in the
course'.[17]

We may allow Dr. Johnson his joke. But, as we look back on Cook's voyages from the viewpoint of the twentieth century, it is natural that their scientific consequences should loom large: the revision and correction of the world map, the enrichment of the pool of hydrographic information available to navigators, the proving of new techniques of observation and recording, the immense increase in observed data of various sciences, recorded in their geographical setting, a more comprehensive view of mankind and its habitat, comparative methods of studying and analysing regional differences. About these fruits of the voyages I shall speak later. But, before European science could profit by them, the records had to be brought back in Cook's ships. If, when he warped *Endeavour* off the Barrier Reef, a piece of coral 'as large as a man's fist' had not lodged in the hole, like a bung, the charting of New Zealand and the east coast of Australia would have had to be redone by another explorer, all the scientists' observations would have been wasted, and there would have been no later voyages under Cook's command. Suppose that the *Resolution* and *Discovery* had gone ashore in the eastern Aleutians or off Icy Cape (as they very nearly did), and suppose that they had been lost without trace like La Pérouse. With them would have disappeared the record of the discovery of Hawaii and the survey of the Pacific seaboard of North America. It was the captain's first and overriding responsibility to bring his ship and her complement safely home. (On one occasion, off the New Zealand coast, this brought Cook the commander and Banks the scientist into conflict.)

The scientific achievements of Cook's expeditions rested on a triumph of seamanship and leadership, without which they would have been sterile. Cook as a seaman still awaits study by an expert hand; of the biographers, Commander Villiers— as we might expect—does most for him.[18] The hazards incurred in navigating a sailing ship over so many thousands of miles of uncharted waters and coasts, in new and unfamiliar hydrologic and meteorological conditions, are difficult for a landsman to apprehend. Before the *Endeavour*'s voyage, Cook had presumably never met a coral reef in soundings, with its peculiar and (for the navigator) unpleasant profile; such a reef, he wrote, was 'scarcely known in Europe'. Certainly he was surprised in the morning of 11 June 1770, after sailing in deep water (over 17 fathom) for an hour, 'when . . . before the Man at the lead could heave another cast the Ship Struck'.

It is not less difficult, except perhaps for hydrographers, to appreciate fully the degree and kind of judgement required of a commander under sail who must 'keep the coast aboard' to satisfy his purposes of exploration and survey, yet without putting his ship into inadmissible risk. Reading his journals leaves us with the impression that Cook often accepted pretty long odds, as he himself confessed. His vindication is the survival of his ships and the remarkable confidence which he inspired in his officers and men. 'In times of the greatest danger', wrote Heinrich Zimmermann, a seaman in the *Discovery*, '. . . his chief concern was to keep calmness and order on the ship. In this he was so successful that for the most part all eyes were fixed on him.'[19] Cook himself, with his distaste for unnecessary drama, was inclined to soft-pedal talk about danger. Real dangers and hardships, he wrote, occurred on such voyages 'often enough to give the mind sufficient anxiety', without men adding 'others which hardly ever had existence but in their imaginations'.

Yet Cook was not a phlegmatic man. As Dr. Beaglehole has said, he does not strew around keys to his heart; but here and there in the journals he opens the door just a little and lets us look through. He can write of 'the very jaws of distruction' in which his ship found herself off the Barrier Reef; of 'the Vicissitudes [which] . . . must always attend an unknown Navigation'. He can describe this service as 'unsuportable'— 'was it not for the pleasure which naturly results to a Man from being the first discoverer'. Danger crops up quite 'often enough' in the journals to suggest the qualities of foresight, promptness in reaction, resourcefulness, and (in short) professional competence that enabled the commander to cope with it and to survive.

In 1772, while the choice of ships for the second voyage by Cook was under discussion, Admiral Palliser—perhaps with some help from Cook in composition—wrote a perceptive paper entitled 'Thoughts upon the Kind of Ships proper to be employed on Discoveries in distant parts of the Globe'.[20] For this service, he held, the ship 'must be of a large Burthen, and of a small Draught of Water, with a Body that will bear to take the Ground, and of a Size which . . . may be safely and conveniently laid on shore'. 'In such a Vessel', he went on, 'an able Sea Officer will be more venturesome and better enabled to fulfill his Instructions . . .' Palliser instanced the success of the *Endeavour*: it was 'these properties in her . . . that enabled Capt Cook to stay in those Seas so much longer than any other Ship ever did or could do: and altho' Discovery was not the first Object of his Voyage, it enabled him to traverse far greater Space of Seas, before then unnavigated: to discover great Tracts of Country . . . and even to explore and survey the extensive Coasts of those new discovered Countries; in short it was those Properties of the Ship, with Capt Cook's great Diligence, Perseverance & Resolution during the Voyage, that enabled him to discover so much more, and at greater Distance than any Discoverer performed before during One Voyage, and has very deservedly gained him the Reputation of an able Seaman, an Artist and a good Officer . . .'. Palliser's paper was a riposte to Mr. Banks's animadversions on the Navy Board's plans for the expedition, and the sting comes in its tail: 'The Business of Discovery, the Care & Navigation of the Ships and conducting of every thing relative to the Undertaking, must ever depend on the King's Sea Officers only, they being chosen Men, fit for it.'

Without dissenting from Palliser's conclusion, we may remark that, by 1768, Cook had spent almost as many years in the merchant service as in the Royal Navy. The North Sea trade was reckoned by a contemporary to be the 'best nursery for seamen'.[21] The need of 'nurseries for seamen', in a vigorous merchant navy and fishing fleet, has been a vital element in British polity since the sixteenth century; Cook is perhaps their most splendid alumnus. Seamanship is doubtless best learnt young. Cook's experience in Whitby shipping before 1755 certainly taught him the principles of pilotage, even if it gave him little practice in deep-sea navigation. It was presumably then that he developed the instinctive seamanship, enabling him to 'smell land', which impressed his men in the Pacific. As the fo'c's'le gossip in his ships went, 'when no one else had a suspicion of danger he often came up on deck and changed the course of the ship because land was near'; and 'occasions were frequent when he alone was sensible of the existence of land, and he was always right'.[22] From the inshore navigation with the lead, among the banks and swatchways of the North Sea, he must have learnt (in the words of his editor) 'to view a shoal with equanimity'. These were important lessons for an explorer and surveyor who must judge just how far he could venture inshore in uncharted waters and must divine the trend of an inaccessible coastline.

Two years after enlisting in the Navy, Cook got his master's certificate from the Trinity House; and this was to be his rating for the next eleven years (1757–68), for five of them in larger ships—men-of-war of up to seventy guns—than he had yet sailed in. If we consider (on paper!) the master's duties under naval regulations, the selection of Cook (in succession) for the Newfoundland survey and for command of the *Endeavour* may seem less arbitrary. The master was the senior executive officer of the ship, responsible for her navigation and seaworthiness. By virtue of this (as Professor Lewis has noted)[23] he steadily advanced in ship-status during the eighteenth century.

Navigation of the ship involved the taking of soundings, selection of passages and anchorages, and marking of hazards. Cook's Pacific journals show him time and again sending away his master on these necessary jobs. The extent to which a master went beyond the call of duty to tackle a coastal survey depended on his personal qualities and on the opportunities his captain gave him. Cook observed (in 1770) that he did not know many seamen who were 'Capable of drawing a Chart or sketch of a Sea Coast'; and a glance at the charts of George Robertson, master of the ship in which Captain Wallis had discovered Tahiti in 1766, bears out this stricture.[24] In 1758 and 1759 pilotage of the St. Lawrence, from which the French had removed all aids to navigation, in preparation for the assault on Quebec showed Cook the need for charting; and with Captain Simcoe's encouragement and Holland's tuition he 'brought in his hand'. To a man of Cook's capacious intellect and faculty for precise observation, hydrographic survey must have been peculiarly satisfying. Colville, in 1762, wrote of 'the work [Mr. Cook] has undertaken', implying that Cook had specialized in this part of his duty.

What we have of Cook's hydrographic output before 1763 is nevertheless conventional in character, though of excellent quality. There is the big St. Lawrence chart, there are harbour plans and coastal sketches. There are sailing directions, competent and thorough, cast in the traditional pattern followed in pilot-books of the Renaissance as in Admiralty Pilots today. Cook was to carry with him into the Pacific the recording habits he had formed on the Atlantic coasts of North America. His instructions for working into and out of Halifax or St. John's are closely paralleled, in his Pacific journals, by many passages on pilotage for harbours of the South Sea, of North-West America, or of the sub-Antarctic. The importance that Cook ascribed to written aids to navigation is illustrated by his criticism of Bougainville, in 1773, while in the Tuamotus, 'for not once mentioning the Situation of any one place in his whole run through this Sea' and for failing 'to make the same judicious Nautical remarks he has done in the Straits of Magelhanes'.

In 1762—as in 1768—Cook's superiors obviously knew a lot more about him than we do. As in 1768, again, they may well have been surprised by the consequences of their decision and by its end-product. We too should be surprised if, leaving hindsight aside, we formed our judgement on Cook's abilities in 1762 solely from the documentation available up to this date. It was after all only four years since he had become acquainted with so rudimentary a survey instrument as the plane table. In these years his intellectual growth must have been exceptional. Cook's charting of Newfoundland was effected by the most thorough hydrographic survey yet made by an Englishman overseas, foreshadowing modern practice in conception and execution. As to its method, I confess that some recent published studies now seem to me slightly romantic.[25] This summer, in the track of Cook's survey of 1766, my wife and I traversed the south coast in the weekly C.N.R. steamer. This is a deeply indented fjord-coastline, often with steep-to shores rising sheer from the water to a considerable height. During the summer season, when Cook did his surveying, fog is frequent. In these circumstances, a man of his empirical common sense must have modified any preconceived plan he may have had for regular triangulation from shore stations. In fact, after July 1764, when he began his survey in the north of the island, the journal of the *Grenville* makes no further reference to the measurement of base lines.

However this may be, Cook's survey in five summer seasons (1763–7) produced the best map of the island yet made. Admiralty surveyors of the 1830s and 1870s found his work 'extremely correct', and thought that 'none [of the old charts] can with any degree of safety be trusted by the seaman, excepting those of Cook and Lane'.

Apart from Cook's letters, which show mature powers of expression, the written records of the Newfoundland survey are extremely barren.[26] The logs and journals kept in the *Grenville* contain practically no evidence that, outside St. John's, Newfoundland had any population, any fauna or flora, any scenery worthy of note. What a stark contrast with Cook's Pacific journals! There we have detailed descriptions of the native peoples and their way of life, speculations on their origin and migrations, observation of birds, animals, and vegetation, discussion of economic potentials. Yet the same man produced these very different records. In Newfoundland Cook was contained within the specification of an exacting professional task; his sympathies (as Dr. Beaglehole has remarked) were limited by his experience. But the Pacific voyages, with research in their programme and a retinue of scientific observers, took all knowledge for their province. Contact with men of more varied culture offered a challenge to which Cook's strong and penetrating natural intelligence responded. It opened the eyes of his mind.

I hope that I have not dwelt unduly on Cook's hydrographic work up to 1768. It is not to be underrated as a preparation for his performance in the Pacific. On the contrary, under-standing of Cook the hydrographer seems to me indispens-able for appreciation of Cook the geographical explorer and of his legacy to the modern world. His passion for exact information could not be satisfied unless he were able to describe a discovery, in words and charts, precisely enough to serve the needs of future navigators. As he wrote (in extravagant terms for him), 'the world will hardly admit of an excuse for a man leaving a Coast unexplored he has once discover'd'. The unknown (assuming it to be knowable) was distasteful to him. In pursuit of it, he was impelled 'not only to go farther than any one had done before but as far as it was possible for man to go'. He had to see for himself.

The Pacific Ocean, the theatre of Cook's career in dis-covery, occupies one-third of the earth's surface. Its explora-tion and mapping, before the days of steam, have been controlled by its great extension in longitude, with few fixed points of reference, and by its wind systems. It was difficult of access by Europeans. Voyages of discovery had to be made east to west or west to east, from the point of entry, within narrow lanes of latitude. The immense latitudinal range of the ocean, from south to north, takes in widely different physical environments and harbours a great variety of habitat and life. Before Cook's time, this was almost a closed book to Europeans. It was indeed a 'New World' that he dis-covered—though not in the sense expected by Dalrymple.

Looking at the map of the Pacific today, we can see that its geographical content was, in large measure, established by Cook's exploratory surveys in the ten years 1769–79. They embraced the island groups of Polynesia and southern Mela-nesia; New Zealand and the east coast of Australia; the southern fringe of the ocean, almost to the edge of the Ant-arctic Continent; the Pacific littoral of North America; the sea passages linking the Pacific with other oceans—in the south-east by Le Maire Strait and Cape Horn, in the south-west by Torres Strait, in the north by Bering Strait. Cook's great traverses of the Pacific—east and west in high and low latitudes, north and south—swept away the mythical elements which had long haunted its cartography and exploration. In Polynesia, when his voyages were over, only a handful of islands remained undiscovered. But more important than the scope of Cook's surveys was their accuracy. Any subsequent navigator using his charts had no excuse for failing to find an island which Cook had discovered.

It is of course true that his hydrographic methods in the Pacific had to be different from those he had used in Newfoundland. On the Pacific voyages, Cook was far from his base and bound by time, season, and logistics—yet he had an extensive geographical programme in his orders. He had to put speed first. In Newfoundland he had surveyed 2,000 miles of intricate coastline in five summer seasons (say 25 months)—by no means slow work. Yet on the first Pacific voyage the coasts of New Zealand (2,400 miles) were charted in six months; on the second, the New Hebrides group, covering six degrees of latitude, was surveyed in six weeks; on the third, 3,000 miles of the North American seaboard in four months. These were exploratory surveys, done mainly by coastal traverse with observations from the ship; only rarely could Cook get his instruments ashore. He did not like this compromise with his standards; 'the word survey', he wrote in the New Hebrides, 'is not to be understood here in its literal sense.' Nevertheless, his outlines and fixes were good enough to be adopted on Admiralty charts of the nineteenth century.

Cook's surveys in the Pacific are now superseded as authorities for navigation. They retain their value as ecological tools. The expeditions brought back to Europe a wealth of new data in the natural and social sciences. To the

location and distribution of these material, hiss precise charting provides an essential geographical key. Comparative
studies by the biologist or the sociologist are concerned with
factors of environment, location, distribution, and flow. They
depend on accurate and correctly designed maps. From this
point of view, the geographical coverage of Cook's exploratory voyages is not more significant than the fact that they
were completed within a very narrow time-span, serving as
a chronological point of origin for modern studies. His mapping of the discoveries complements other materials—the
descriptions, the drawings, the specimens—in furnishing a
precious ecological record, or vertical cross-section, of the
Pacific and its life at a particular point in time.

Very early in the sixteenth century, Europeans were looking
eastward and westward across the Pacific. Before the end of
the century they had theoretical answers to the main questions raised by its geography. These answers were not to be
tested by experience for another 200 years, for want of im-
pulse and for want of technique. Without a reliable means
for ascertaining his longitude at sea, not knowing the drift of
his ship, the explorer of this immense ocean, with its great
longitudinal spread, could not avoid large errors in estimat-
ing his distance run or telling where he was or where he had
been. The eighteenth century brought the chronometer; and,
as the heir to the scientific revolution of the seventeenth century, this age had the motive and—for the first time—the
tools for collecting observations and specimens in sufficient
quantity to support comparative and inductive analysis.

Cook's work in the Pacific foreshadowed the great increase
in the volume and variety of observed data on which modern
hydrography, oceanography, and meteorology rest. In other
sciences, his expeditions brought back from this virgin field
a profusion of study materials: for the botanist, the zoologist,

the anthropologist, the ethnologist. As a botanist has written, the *Endeavour*'s voyage was 'the first organised and thoroughly equipped voyage of biological exploration'.[27] It is true that Cook carried professional scientists with him on the first and second voyages; but he himself had been infected by Banks with the habits of observation and recording, and he was well served in this field by his surgeons, notably William Anderson. In the journals we see his mind incessantly at work on whatever came under his eyes. If his solutions sometimes seem naïve, it is remarkable that he so often asked the right and necessary questions. The voyaging of the Polynesians is still being discussed in terms formulated by Cook in 1777.[28]

In the history of science, Cook's voyages take their place in the great collecting phase which opened in the eighteenth century. The multiplicity of data accumulated by new techniques could not be digested by the older encyclopedic science. The polymath was superseded by the specialists. The consequences for the study of Cook's work are apparent in the trend of recent literature. We have catalogues of bird-drawings from the voyages, of the shells collected, of the artefacts brought back. Commemorative publications contain papers on the contribution made by Cook's voyages in various fields of science and technology. It has taken a long time to digest the products of Cook's work, and the process is far from completed. Much mere inventorization remains to be done.

The element of scientific inquiry and research is greater in Cook's voyages than in any earlier expeditions. They had of course political—or geopolitical—motives: the search for the Southern Continent, the search for a North-West Passage. They had momentous, if unexpected, political consequences. Australia, New Zealand, and the west coast of North America were to be settled by people of English speech. Of these historical events Cook's voyages of discovery were a proximate cause. But (in the main) the plan, the course, and the fruits of the expeditions reflect the experimental and analytical mind of their commander not less than the intellectual climate of his age.

Take away ten years from Cook's life, and how much poorer the world would have been! Later explorers would have made the geographical discoveries; botanical and zoological specimens and native artefacts would have been collected, brought back to the museums of Europe, and classified; the peoples of Polynesia and the North American coast and their way of life would have been described—though perhaps too late, less intimately, and not without adulteration. If so much was done in so short a time, to the immense advantage of the historical record, it is because, by a happy chance, the right man came up at the right moment.

It is here that evaluation of Cook as a hero must lean on appreciation of Cook as a man. Cook's character, in his last ten years, is reflected most clearly in his personal relationships with the men who served under him and with the native peoples, friendly or hostile, whom he encountered.

To his officers and crew, Cook presented a front of authority, with the reticence which goes with it; of sternness tempered by equity and comprehension; of a concern for their welfare and a command over circumstance which won their confidence and often their admiration. Some of these qualities we can see in the fine Dance portrait at Greenwich, which Mrs. Cook thought too stern. Behind the external facets lay professional ability, cultivated to a high degree by experience and hard thought, and a profound understanding of what he called 'the Tempers and dispossissions of Seamen in general'. Cook himself had messed on the lower deck, in the gunroom, and in the wardroom. He knew (for instance) the instinctive distaste of sailors for any item of diet 'out of the Common way, altho it be ever so much for their good'; he knew, and practised on the knowledge, that as soon as 'they see their Superiors set a Value upon it, it becomes the finest stuff in the World'. For his success in the elimination of scurvy, Cook got a medal from the Royal Society; but the historians of naval medicine now take the view that his 'three voyages actually delayed the introduction of the best anti-scorbutic, lemon-juice, to the Navy'.[29] If so, it was because no later commander was so successful as Cook in enforcing the necessary measures of hygiene by judicious exercise of discipline and comprehension of his men. Cook's leadership has been well characterized by Dr. Beaglehole: 'The humanity that is kindness, understanding, tolerance, wisdom in the treatment of men, a quality practised naturally as well as planned for, is what gave Cook's voyages their success, as much as the soundness of his seamanship and the brilliance of his navigation.'[30] We may compare the impression made by Cook on Fanny Burney: 'the most moderate, humane, and gentle circumnavigator that ever went out upon discoveries'.[31] Her father however found him rather abstracted in conversation, as if his mind were elsewhere.

The same qualities of sympathy and recognition of the right of men to be different characterizes Cook's dealings with native peoples. His combination of friendliness and firmness, his success in communication on equal terms, his eager interest in the island societies of Polynesia, in the way in which their people organized their lives, in their manners and customs, and in the reasons for them—all these factors assured the safety of his expeditions. More than this: Cook was able to bring back a priceless record of a way of life that other Europeans were to destroy.

'So skilful', writes a modern anthropologist, 'was he in his relations with most islanders that among many Polynesians his name ("Toote") was remembered and respected for generations.'[32] In Cook's relations with simple men, as we observe them in the pages of Dr. Beaglehole's edition of the Journals, his own character emerges. By a tragic irony, Cook the man met his end at the hand of islanders to whom he was a hero, if not a god.[33]

Notes

1. Daniel Wray, in 1777.

2. Captain James King, in 1784.

3. George Forster, in 1786.

4. The eulogy inscribed on the monument, and also printed in the preliminaries of *A Voyage to the Pacific Ocean* (1784), was attributed by contemporaries to Captain Lord Mulgrave.

5. David Samwell, *A Narrative of the Death of Captain James Cook* (1786), p. 27.

6. J. A. Williamson, *Cook and the Opening of the Pacific* (1946), p. 213.

7. J. C. Beaglehole, 'On the character of Captain James Cook', *Geogr. Journal*, CXXII (1956), p. 418.

8. *The Journals of Captain James Cook*, ed. J. C. Beaglehole, I, p. cclxxxii. (Hereafter cited as *Journals*.)

9. Alexander Dalrymple, *An Historical Collection of . . . Voyages and Discoveries in the South Pacific Ocean* (1770), I, p. xxx.

10. Williamson, p. 103.

11. Andrew Kippis, *The Life of Captain James Cook* (1788); Arthur Kitson, *Captain James Cook, R.N., F.R.S.* (1907); Hugh Carrington, *Life of Captain Cook* (1939).

12. *Journals*, I, p. cxiii.

13. Michael Lewis, *The Navy of Britain* (1948), p. 271.

14. Holland's letter (11 January 1792) to Simcoe's son, John Graves Simcoe, Lieutenant-Governor of Upper Canada, was printed in *The Mariner's Mirror*, XL (1954), pp. 97–8. Perhaps in consequence of it, the name Cook Bay, bestowed by the Lieutenant-Governor, is to be found in the south of Lake Simcoe on the modern map.

15. Admiralty to Navy Board, 12 February 1767 (National Maritime Museum, ADM/B/126).

16. Cf. *The Newfoundland Journal of Aaron Thomas* [1794–5], ed. J. M. Murray (1968), pp. 59–62; also *Journals*, II, p. 955.

17. *Boswell's Life*, ed. Birkbeck Hill, II (1934), pp. 147–8.

18. Alan Villiers, *Captain Cook: the Seaman's Seaman* (1967).

19. H. Zimmermann, *Zimmermann's Account of the Third Voyage of Captain Cook*, trans. U. Tewsley (1926), p. 42.

20. Printed in *Journals*, II, pp. 709–11.

21. Henry Taylor (of North Shields), *Memoirs* (1811), p. 3.

22. Zimmermann, p. 41.

23. Lewis, pp. 174–5.

24. Robertson's charts are in the Hydrographic Department, Ministry of Defence.

25. For instance R. A. Skelton, *James Cook, Surveyor of Newfoundland* (San Francisco, 1965).

26. Some letters of Cook are in the Graves MSS., National Maritime Museum (ADM/B/126); the *Grenville's* journals in the P.R.O. (Adm 52/1263).

27. W. T. Stearn, 'The botanical results of the *Endeavour* voyage', *Endeavour*, no. 100 (1968), p. 3.

28. Cf. Andrew Sharp, *Ancient Voyagers in the Pacific* (1956), chap. 1.

29. This conclusion is reached by C. C. Lloyd and J. L. S. Coulter, *Medicine and the Navy*, vol. II (1961). The quotation is from W. E. Snell, 'Captain Cook's surgeons', *Medical History*, VII (1963), p. 54.

30. J. C. Beaglehole, 'On the character of Captain James Cook', p. 425.

31. Fanny Burney, *Diary and Letters*, I (1904), p. 318.

32. Douglas L. Oliver, *The Pacific Islands*, rev. edn. (1961), p. 96.

33. *Journals*, III, pp. cxliii–cxliv.

I A Master, R.N., in the 18th century: pen drawing in the remark-book of Alexander Hamilton, *c.* 1762.

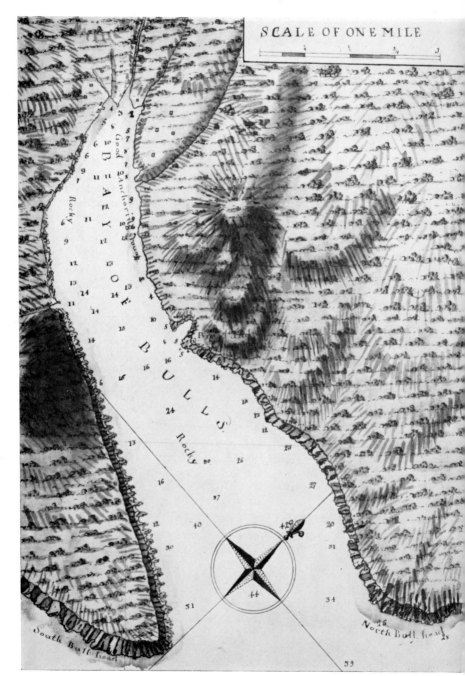

II   A harbour plan drawn by Cook in 1763, as master of H.M.S. *Northumberland*.

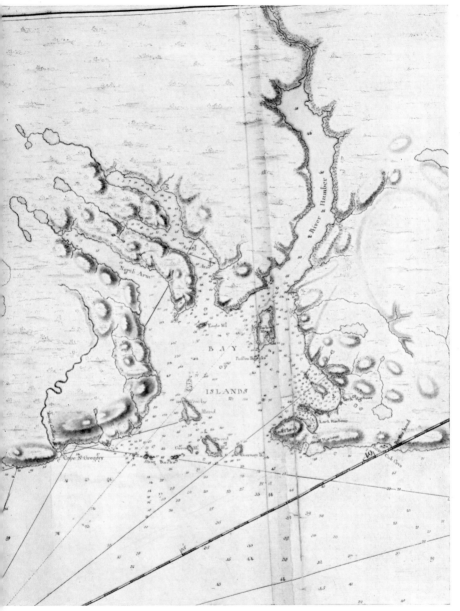

III   Cook's charting of Newfoundland: detail from his MS. chart of the west coast,
surveyed in 1767.

Week Day	Month Day	Winds	Remarkable Occurrences on board His Majestys Bark Endeavour, River Thames —
May 1768 Friday 27 to Friday July 29		NbW	Moderate and fair weather, at 11 am hoisted the Pendant and took charge of the Ship agreeable to my Commission of the 25th Instant. She lying in the Bason in Deptford yard. From this day to the 21st of July we were constantly employed in fitting the Ship taking on board Stores and Provisions &c&c the which day we said from Deptford and anchored in Galleons reach where we remained untill the 30th. The transactions of each day both whilst we lay here and at Deptford are inserted in the Logg Book and as they contain nothing but common occurrences it was thought not necessary to [insert them] here —
July 30 to Augt 7			Saturday July 30th Weighd from Galleons, ditto the wind at E, and made sail down the River, the same day anchord at Gravesend, and the next morning weighd from thence, and at Noon anchord at the Buoy of the Fairway— on Wednesday 3d of August anchord in the Downs in 9 fathom water Deal castle N.WbW. On Sunday the 7th I Joined the Ship, discharged the Pilot and the next day sailed for Plymouth—
Monday 8		NbW	Fresh breeze and cloudy weather the most part of these 24 hours at 10 am weighd and came to sail at Noon the South
		SWbS	Foreland bore N.E.½.N. distant 6 or 7 miles —
Tuesday 9		NW to North	Gentle breezes and cloudy weather at 7 pm the Tide being against us anchored in 13 fathom water Dungeness SWbW — at 11 weighd and made sail down channell at Noon Beachey head N.N.E.½.E. distant 6 Leagues Lat observed 50..30 North
Wednesday 10		NWbW NEbE	Variable light airs and clear weather at 8 pm Beachey head N.E.bE distant 4 Leagues, and at 8 am it bore N.E.bN. 9 Leagues. found the Variation of the Compass to be 20° West at Noon the Isle of Wight N.W.bW—
Thursday 11		Varble	Light airs and clear weather at 8 pm Dunnose N.bW 5 Leagues and at 6 am it bore N.N.E.½.E. distt 5 Leagues
Wednesday 12		Easterly	Light airs and Calms all these 24 hours— at Noon the Bill of Portland bore N.W.bN distant 3 Leagues Lat obsd 50..24 North —
Thursday 13		Varble	Dc Weather. at Noon the Start Point West 7 or 8 miles Lat observd 50..13 North which must be the Lat of the Start as it bore West —

IV   The first page of Cook's holograph journal in the *Endeavour*, 27 May–13 August 1768.

V   Joseph Banks after the voyage of the *Endeavour*: mezzotint by J. R. Smith, published 15 April 1773, after a portrait by Benjamin West. Banks is depicted in a Maori cloak, with Polynesian artefacts grouped round him.

VI   The *Endeavour* at sea: pencil drawing by Sydney Parkinson.

VII   One Tree Hill and Matavai Bay, Tahiti: pen and wash drawing by Parkinson. The *Endeavour* lay at anchor here 13 April–13 July 1769; in the foreground is a coral tree.

A VIEW of the WATERING PLACE at TOLAGA

IX   Double canoe of Raiatea, Society Islands: wash drawing. In the background, other sailing canoes; on the right, three reef herons.

X Cook encountering Maoris in Queen Charlotte Sound, New Zealand, February 1777: water colour drawing by John Webber. The *Resolution* and *Adventure* are at anchor in the Sound.

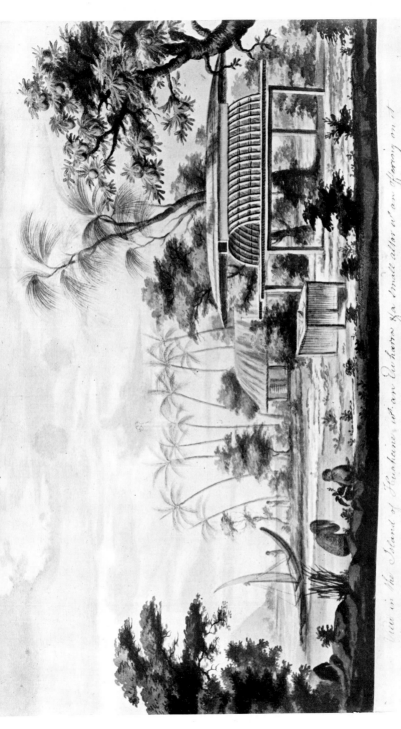

View in the Island of Huahine with an Enharee for trade altar with an offering on it

XI View in Huahine, Society Islands, 17–20 July 1769: pen and wash drawing signed 'Sydney Parkinson pinx^t Australia 1770'. On the right, beneath a breadfruit tree, is the *fare atua* ('house of the god'), with an offering; the tall tree behind is *casuarina equisetifolia*, with coconut trees in the background.

XII (above) The *Resolution* off the South Sandwich Islands, 31 January 1775: wash drawing by Joseph Gilbert.

XIII (below) The *Resolution* and *Discovery* in Snug Corner Cove, Alaska, 12-15 May 1778: wash drawing by John Webb

XIV (*above*)   Cook's meeting with the Chukchi at St. Lawrence Bay, Siberia, 10 August 1778: wash drawing by Webber.
XV (*below*)   The *Resolution* and *Discovery* in Avacha Bay (Petropavlovsk), Kamchatka, 28 April–16 June 1779, with the portable observatory ashore under guard: inset of Edward Riou's MS. chart of Avacha Bay.

The Resolution beating through the Ice, with the Discovery in the most imminent Danger in the Background.

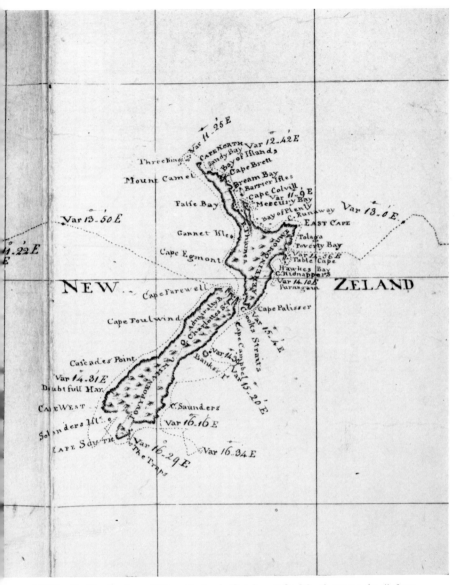

XVII   Cook's charting of New Zealand, October 1769–March 1770: detail from his MS. 'Chart of the Great South Sea . . . shewing the Track and Discoveries made by the Endeavour Bark . . .'

XVI (*opposite*)   'The *Resolution* beating through the Ice, with the *Discovery* in the most eminent danger in the Distance': wash drawing by Webber. Off Icy Cape (70° 19′ N, 161° 41′ W), on 18 August 1778, the ships 'were in shoald water upon a lee shore and the main-body of the ice to windward driving down upon us'.

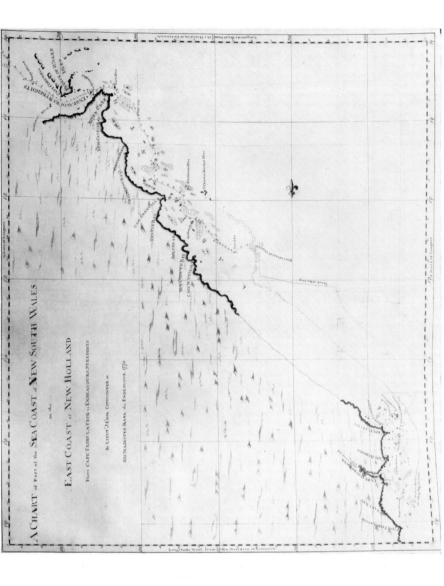

XVIII The Great Barrier Reef, showing the reef where the *Endeavour* struck, 11 June 1770; and Endeavour's River where she lay